DATE DUE

LUKE APPLING

FRANK THOMAS

DOC WHITE

DICK ALLEN

MINNIE MINOSO

MAGGLIO ORDOÑEZ

ED WALSH

LUIS APARICIO

EARLY WYNN

JOE JACKSON

CARLTON FISK

NELLIE FOX

THE HISTORY OF THE
CHICAGO
WHITE SOX

WAYNE STEWART

CREATIVE ☙ EDUCATION

C 1   2003   17.95

Published by Creative Education, 123 South Broad Street, Mankato, MN 56001

Creative Education is an imprint of The Creative Company.

Designed by Rita Marshall.

Photographs by AllSport (Jonathan Daniel, Otto Greule Jr.), Associated Press/Wide World Photos,

Icon Sports Media (David Seelig), Sports Gallery (Al Messerschmidt), SportsChrome (Jeff Carlick,

Jonathan Kirn, Michael Zito), TimePix (Thomas S. England)

Library of Congress Cataloging-in-Publication Data

Stewart, Wayne, 1951- The history of the Chicago White Sox / by Wayne Stewart.

p. cm. — (Baseball)   ISBN 1-58341-204-2

Summary: Highlights the key personalities and memorable games in the history of the

team that was founded by Charles Comiskey in 1901.

1. Chicago White Sox (Baseball team)—History—

Juvenile literature. [1. Chicago White Sox (Baseball team)—History.

2. Baseball—History.] 1. Title. II. Baseball (Mankato, Minn.).

GV875.C58 S84 2002   796.357'64'0977311—dc21   2001047855

First Edition 9 8 7 6 5 4 3 2 1

CHICAGO,

ILLINOIS, IS A BUSTLING METROPOLIS SITUATED ON THE

flatlands of the Midwest. This mighty city—known for its steady

winds and towering skyscrapers—was practically destroyed when

the Great Chicago Fire of 1871 leveled more than 11,000 buildings.

But Chicago quickly rebuilt, and today it boasts a population of just

under three million people.

Chicago is also home to a professional baseball team called the

White Sox, which was a charter member of the American League

(AL) when the league was formed in 1901. Originally, the team's

owner, Charles Comiskey, announced that the squad would be

known as the White Stockings. However, to save space in their

columns, local newspaper writers began referring to the team as the

DOC WHITE

White Sox, and the name stuck.

{EARLY SUCCESS...AND SCANDAL} It didn't take long for

| The Sox played in Minnesota for seven seasons (as the St. Paul Saints) before settling in Chicago. | the White Sox, who played on the south side of Chicago, to win their first pennant. The first official AL game took place between Chicago and the Cleveland Indians on April 24, 1901. Five months later, the White Sox won it all. Back then, winning the |

pennant was the ultimate success story since the World Series didn't

exist until 1903.

Pitcher Doc White starred for Chicago from 1903 through 1913.

He won 159 games for the Sox over that span, posting a sparkling

2.28 career ERA. Decades later, White would be named to Chicago's

"Team of the Century," a list of greats selected in the year 2000 to

celebrate 100 years of White Sox baseball.

The team won another pennant in 1906, then faced the

PAUL KONERKO

In his last big-league season (**1920**), "Shoeless" Joe Jackson batted .382 with 121 RBI.

JOE JACKSON

crosstown Cubs in the only all-Chicago World Series ever. The White Sox were called the "Hitless Wonders" by sportswriters because only two of their batters hit above the .260 mark. Still, the Sox managed to win the AL crown with fine pitching and defense, then brought home their first world championship by knocking off the Cubs in six games.

Fleet-footed infielder Eddie Collins led the league in stolen bases in **1919**, **1923**, and **1924**.

One of the heroes of the 1906 World Series was pitcher Ed Walsh, who won two games in the series. Walsh only got better in the seasons that followed. In 1908, he recorded a club-record 40 wins, and two seasons later he posted a 1.27 ERA, still the lowest ever by a White Sox pitcher.

After a number of mediocre seasons, the White Sox charged to a franchise-best 100–54 record in 1917. Perhaps the brightest star on that team was pitcher Red Farber. In that year's World Series against

EDDIE COLLINS

New Comiskey Park, which replaced the old park in **1991**, was built at a cost of $137 million.

COMISKEY PARK

the New York Giants, Farber notched three victories as the Sox won

the title again in six games.

Chicago captured another AL pennant in 1919, this time behind the heroics of pitcher Eddie Cicotte, who won 29 games for the Sox. Another standout was outfielder "Shoeless" Joe Jackson, who compiled a .356 career batting average, the second-highest ever in big-league play. No less an authority than legendary Detroit Tigers outfielder Ty Cobb once called Jackson "the finest natural hitter in the history of the game."

But from the very start of the first World Series game in 1919, Chicago committed numerous suspicious-looking errors. It was later discovered that eight of the White Sox players had accepted bribes from gamblers to lose the series on purpose so that the gamblers could make money. The ugly incident became known as the

EDDIE CICOTTE

"Black Sox Scandal." Cicotte, one of the players who accepted

bribes, lost two games in the Series. "I have played a crooked game,"

he said regretfully, "and I have lost."

{THE DRY SPELL BEGINS} In 1921, Kenesaw Landis, baseball's

first commissioner, punished the eight "Black Sox" players by ban-

ning them from baseball for life. That included Jackson, even though he appeared to have played to win in the 1919 World Series—posting a team-best .375 batting average—and maintained his innocence until the day he died.

After the scandal, the White Sox seemed to be jinxed; they would not return to the World Series for 40 years. Still, such splendid players as pitcher Ted Lyons did give fans at Chicago's Comiskey Park plenty

to cheer about in the 1920s. Lyons spent 21 seasons in a Sox uniform and twice led the AL in wins despite mediocre run support from the Chicago offense. The Hall-of-Famer racked up a team-record 260 victories over the course of his career.

The next Sox star, shortstop Luke Appling, made his debut in 1930. He played in Chicago through 1950, winning two batting crowns and establishing himself as the team's all-time leader in five major categories, including hits, doubles, and runs scored. Appling

FRANK THOMAS

was famous for his uncanny bat control. Often, he would purposely

foul off one nasty pitch after another, waiting to get a pitch that he

could hit with authority.

By 1932, new team owner J. Louis Comiskey grew tired of the

Sox's pennant drought. In an effort to revive the club, he bought a

handful of players from the Philadelphia Athletics for $150,000—

an astronomical amount of money in those days. The two biggest names he acquired were infielder Jimmy Dykes and slugging outfielder Al Simmons. Simmons earned his paycheck, hitting above .330 in 1933 and 1934, but it wasn't enough. The White Sox continued to lose.

In the years after Dykes became Chicago's manager (1934), the team continued to feature some top-notch talent. Powerful first baseman Zeke Bonura averaged 110 RBI per season in the mid-1930s, and pitcher Thornton Lee gave the team some strong performances in the '40s. Still, the Sox remained mired in the middle of the AL standings.

{THE GO-GO '50s} In the 1950s, the White Sox got their fans excited again by employing a new, aggressive style of play. Fans started calling the team the "Go-Go" Sox and encouraged its speedy players to run wild on the base paths. During the 12 seasons

In **1933**, Al Simmons played in the first All-Star Game, which was held in Comiskey Park.

17

AL SIMMONS

Like Minnie
Minoso,
Ray Durham
was a solid
defender and
top-notch
base stealer.

between 1951 and 1962, a White Sox player led the AL in stolen

bases 11 times. The first great base burglar of that era was outfielder

Between **1958** and **1970**, Luis Aparicio won seven Gold Glove awards for his great fielding.

Minnie Minoso, a fan favorite who topped the AL in

steals three seasons in a row.

Brilliant defensive shortstop Luis Aparicio was the

next extraordinary base stealer. From 1956 through

1962, he led the league in steals every season, swiping

20   a high of 56 in 1959. As the scrappy Sox ran their opponents

ragged, it began paying off in victories. From 1951 to 1967, the

White Sox chalked up 17 consecutive winning seasons, the third-

best such streak in AL history.

On the mound, hard-throwing Billy Pierce was the team's ace

during that era, leading the White Sox in victories almost every sea-

son. Second baseman Nellie Fox also contributed to Chicago's excit-

ing, free-wheeling style by slapping hits all over the diamond. He

LUIS APARICIO

led the AL in hits four times in the 1950s and won the AL Most

Valuable Player (MVP) award in 1959. The feisty, 5-foot-9 Fox was

a sure-handed defender as well and teamed up with Aparicio to

form a sensational double-play combination.

Pitchers Hoyt Wilhelm and Early Wynn were also key names

in Chicago in the 1950s. Wilhelm was known for his fluttering knuckleball, and Wynn was a fierce competitor who often became downright hostile when staring down opposing batters. He enjoyed

his greatest season in 1959, topping the AL in wins with 23 and capturing the Cy Young Award at the age of 39. "A pitcher has to look at the hitter as his mortal enemy," Wynn said in explanation of his success.

After finishing in second place in 1957 and 1958, the

White Sox captured the 1959 AL pennant, finally ending their long dry spell. Unfortunately, after cruising to a 94–60 record during the season, the Sox came up short in the World Series, losing to the Los Angeles Dodgers in six contests.

{STARS SHINE, BUT NO PENNANTS FLY} From 1960 to 1983, a parade of great players came and went in Chicago, but no more championship banners were raised. Knuckleball pitcher Wilbur Wood joined the White Sox in 1967. Although knuckleball

BILLY PIERCE

Slick-fielding third baseman Robin Ventura helped the White Sox rise at last in the **'90s**.

ROBIN VENTURA

specialists tend to be right-handers, Wood was a lefty. Because

throwing knucklers is easy on a pitcher's arm, he could throw virtu-

ally every day. In 1968, he worked in a staggering 88

games and was named the Relief Pitcher of the Year

by *The Sporting News*. He soon became a starter

instead and remained a top hurler into the 1970s.

In 1972, first baseman Dick Allen almost single-

handedly lifted the Sox to a second-place finish in the AL Western

Division (the league was split into two divisions in 1969). He drilled

37 home runs and collected 70 extra-base hits—more than enough

to earn him the AL MVP award. "Allen is so strong, he has arms like

legs," said Montreal Expos manager Gene Mauch.

Third baseman Bill Melton was also a major source of power

for the Sox in the early 1970s. In 1971, he led all AL batters with

33 home runs. "Those two [Allen and Melton] are murder," griped

A savvy team leader, Hall of Fame catcher Carlton Fisk spent 14 seasons with the White Sox.

CARLTON FISK

Oakland Athletics manager Dick Williams. "Our guys just hate

facing them."

In the early 1980s, two new players joined the White Sox and

quickly became fan favorites: outfielder Harold Baines and catcher

Carlton Fisk. Baines was a clutch hitter who drove in nearly 1,000

runs and smacked 221 home runs before bringing his Chicago career to an end. Fisk, meanwhile, gave the team steady veteran leadership and cranked out more career home runs (351) than any other catcher in baseball history. The durable Fisk also set a new major-league record for games caught. "Success has no shortcut," he said in explanation of his durability, "only a high price of pain and humiliation."

In 1983, manager Tony La Russa guided the White Sox to the AL West title. Chicago went 99–63 that season, winning the division by a whopping 20 games over the second-place Kansas City Royals. Unfortunately, the Sox ran into a red-hot Baltimore Orioles team in the playoffs and were eliminated.

{MORE TITLES AND A CENTENNIAL} The White Sox steadily declined in the late 1980s, then spent the early part of the '90s assembling the pieces of a pennant contender. One such player was reliever Bobby Thigpen, who led the league in saves in 1990.

Harold Baines enjoyed perhaps his finest season in **1985**, batting .309 and driving in 113 runs.

HAROLD BAINES

But no Sox player loomed larger than first baseman Frank Thomas.

Known as the "Big Hurt," Thomas combined brute strength with

In **1993**, Tim Raines ran up an AL record by sliding in safely on 40 straight base-stealing attempts.

a great eye at the plate, which resulted in tons of

home runs and walks. He hit a combined 79 home

runs in 1993 and 1994, winning the AL MVP award

both years. "It's not fair for a guy to be that strong and

yet so disciplined at the plate," said Toronto Blue Jays

28   pitcher Jack Morris. "I have no idea how to get him out."

In 1993, the Sox won another division title but fell to the Blue

Jays in the AL Championship Series (ALCS). In 1994, the Sox were

poised to go even further before a players' strike ended the season

in mid-August. Even though Chicago led the AL Central Division,

there would be no postseason. For the first time since 1904, no World

Series was held, robbing such Sox standouts as Gold Glove-winning

third baseman Robin Ventura and speedy outfielder Tim Raines of

TIM RAINES

a shot at the world championship.

From 1996 to 1999, the White Sox finished second in the AL Central each season. One of the players most instrumental in Chicago's winning ways was hard-hitting outfielder Magglio Ordoñez. In 2000, Ordoñez won the Silver Slugger award, given each season to the league's top hitters at each of the nine positions.

Rookie outfielder Chris Singleton hit a single, double, triple, and homer (the cycle) in a **1999** game.

Two other standouts in the late '90s were second baseman Ray Durham—a premier base-stealing threat who brought surprising power to the plate—and first baseman Paul Konerko. Behind these players, Chicago surged to the top of the AL Central in 2000, hitting more home runs and scoring more runs than any White Sox team in history.

Over the years, the White Sox have proven to be as resilient as the city they call home. Even though the team hasn't won a

CHRIS SINGLETON

Star right
fielder Magglio
Ordoñez
averaged
119 RBI a
season from
1999 to **2001**.

MAGGLIO ORDOÑEZ

Promising
pitcher Jon
Garland was
part of
a strong
White Sox
rotation.

JON GARLAND

World Series in more than 85 years, an array of Sox standouts over

the years has kept the team in contention more often than not.

The hardworking White Sox—the first team to win an AL pennant

more than a century ago—hope to soon raise more banners in the

winds of Chicago.